Coping *with* Anxiety *workbook*

Facilitator Reproducible Guided Self-Exploration Activities

Ester R.A. Leutenberg
& John J. Liptak, Ed.D.

Illustrated by Amy L. Brodsky, LISW-S

101 W. 2nd St., Suite 203
Duluth MN 55802

800-247-6789

books@wholeperson.com
www.wholeperson.com

Coping with Anxiety Workbook
Facilitator Reproducible Guided Self-Exploration Activities

Printed in the United States of America

10 9 8 7 6 5 4 3 2 1

Editorial Director: Carlene Sippola
Art Director: Joy Morgan Dey

Library of Congress Control Number: 2011927798
ISBN: 978-1-57025-256-3

Using This Book

Anxiety is becoming increasingly prevalent in our modern society. Research indicates that the number of people suffering from anxiety disorders continues to increase and this increase in anxiety disorders can be tied to several societal trends:

- The pace of modern life has increased dramatically in recent decades, and research suggests that this pace will continue to increase. People feel the need to increase the pace at which they do things compared with past generations. Most people live their lives in a constant state of doing rather than simply being. Because of this, many people deprive themselves of appropriate sleep and rest, and they eat foods that do not contain the appropriate nutrients necessary for their good health.

- Along with the rapid pace of life, people are exposed to monumental technological, social, occupational and environmental changes. This rate of change is so overpowering that many people do not feel they have time to adjust and assimilate the changes into their lives; thus they face increasing anxiety each day.

- People lack agreement on a set of social values and standards that results in uncertainty about how to live life. Because of an increase in divergent worldviews, globalization and standards portrayed by the media, people are forced to create their own meanings in life and develop their own set of moral values by which to live. When people are unable to find meaning in their lives, they usually turn to less socially acceptable methods for making meaning. This lack of meaning leaves people feeling anxious.

- People often feel less connected than previous generations. When people feel less connected to themselves, their family, others in the community, or even a higher power, they feel disconnected and alienated. This alienation leads people to perceive threats to their well-being and security.

- The way that people work has changed dramatically. Many people have been downsized as corporations attempt to operate on tighter budgets and move operations to countries where the cost of labor is less expensive and the people who are able to hold onto their jobs feel anxious about their job-security. People then feel competitive, with the need to work even harder and longer to maintain their current positions.

There are many trends and forces at work that contribute to feelings of fear and anxiety in people. Fear and anxiety are experiences that are familiar to everyone, but many people often have a serious problem with anxiety at some point in their lives. This book provides assessments and self-guided activities to help people learn effective skills for coping with all forms of anxiety. A variety of self-exploration activities are provided for you to determine which best suit the unique needs of your participants.

Information About Anxiety

Anxiety is a complex, multifaceted experience which contains a combination of different, yet interrelated elements. Anxiety affects us:

- **PHYSICAL:** Anxiety causes a variety of somatic symptoms such as dry mouth, chest pains, lump in throat, temperature change, loss of appetite, headaches, irregular heartbeat, shortness of breath, perspiring, etc.

- **COGNITIVE:** Anxiety is sparked through patterns of distorted thinking. Some of these distorted thought patterns include negative and fearful self-talk, catastrophic thinking, overgeneralization of outcomes based on a single event, and all-or-nothing thinking.

- **EMOTIONAL:** Anxiety is a strong, overwhelming feeling which, in turn, leads to other feelings such as fear, sadness and helplessness.

- **BEHAVIORAL:** Anxiety affects what people do and how they live their lives. Anxiety is effective when it is used to promote evasive action in the threat of danger. The problem arises, however, when peoples' appraisals are out of proportion to a "true" threat and evasive actions are both unnecessary and unhelpful.

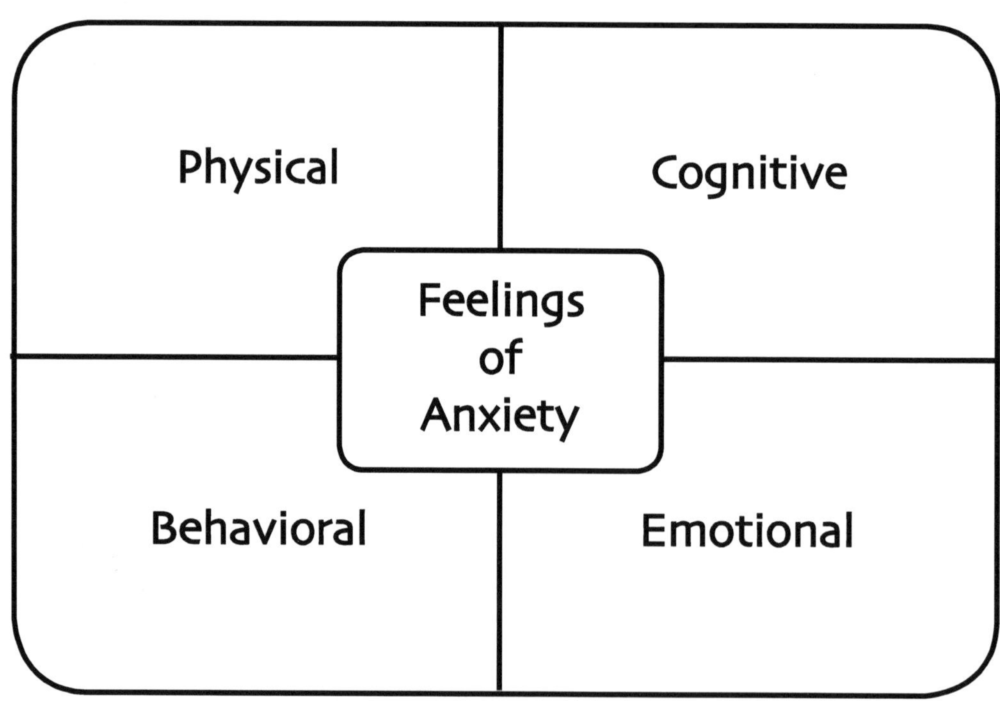

What Is and Is Not Anxiety?

It is important for you as the facilitator to know the differences between anxiety and anxiety disorders. Facilitators can help their participants by reminding them of these facts:

1. **Everyone experiences anxiety.** Everyone has feelings of anxiety in daily life. It is important and life-changing to be able to cope with anxiety and manage it effectively.
2. **Anxiety is normal.** In many situations it is appropriate to act with some anxiety. A lack of feelings of anxiety in certain situations would not be normal. For example, a person who felt some anxiety after being fired would be exhibiting a normal, ordinary reaction. However, when this anxiety becomes so intense that it affects the person's work, relationships and/or whole life, the person is experiencing an unusual amount of anxiety.
3. **Anxiety is a reaction.** This reaction can be managed effectively. By completing the activities and exercises included in this workbook, people will be able to make their lives less anxiety-filled, regardless of the nature and intensity of difficult situations.
4. **Anxiety has many roots**. There is no one cause of anxiety. Anxiety can be caused by a biological or physiological imbalance in the brain, heredity, parenting, early trauma, physical and/or sexual abuse, neglect, recreational drug use, etc.

People experience a variety of anxiety reactions:

- **Situational Anxiety** – This occurs when you worry in the present about an everyday situation like going to the dentist or being in a large group.
- **Fear** – This occurs when you are afraid of an external object or situation that you face such as failing an employee evaluation or being rejected by another person.
- **Phobia** – This is an irrational fear in which you persistently begin to avoid an object or a situation like continuing to take the steps rather than riding in an elevator.
- **Anticipatory Anxiety** – This occurs when you are anxious about something that might occur in the future such as anxiety about an upcoming doctor's appointment. This type of anxiety can quickly turn into a panic attack.
- **Anxiety Disorders** – These disorders occur when normal anxiety becomes more intense than usual, lasts longer than usual (may persist for months), and leads to phobias that detract from life. A client who appears to suffer from an anxiety disorder should be advised to consult a medical or psychiatric professional immediately.

Format of Book

The *Coping with Anxiety Workbook* contains assessments and guided self-exploration activities that can be used with a variety of populations to help participants cope more effectively with the various forms of anxiety. Each chapter of this workbook begins with an annotated Table of Contents with notes and examples for the facilitator. Each chapter contains two primary elements: 1) A set of assessments to help participants gather information about themselves in a focused situation, and 2) a set of guided self-exploration activities to help participants process information and learn more effective ways of behaving to cope with anxiety in their lives.

Assessments

Each chapter begins with an assessment that provides participants with valuable information about themselves. These assessments can enhance recognition of effective and ineffective patterns of behavior, identify life skills which are productive and unproductive, and enrich participants' understanding of how they interact with the world. Assessments provide a path to self-discovery through the participants' exploration of their own unique traits and behaviors. The purpose of these assessments is not to "pigeon-hole" people, but to allow them to explore various elements that are critical for coping with anxiety. This book contains *self-assessments* and not *tests*. Traditional tests measure knowledge or right or wrong responses. For the assessments provided in this book, remind participants that there are no right or wrong answers. These assessments ask only for opinions or attitudes about topics related to a variety of coping skills and abilities.

The assessments in this book are based on self-reported data. In other words, the accuracy and usefulness of the information is dependent on the information that participants honestly provide about themselves. All of the assessments in this workbook are designed to be administered, scored, and interpreted by the participants as a starting point for them to begin to learn more about themselves and their coping skills. Remind participants that the assessments are exploratory exercises and not a final determination of abilities. Lastly, the assessments are not a substitute for professional assistance. If you feel any of your participants need more assistance than you can provide, please refer them to an appropriate professional.

As your participants begin the assessments in this workbook give these instructions:

- Take your time. Because there is no time limit for completing the assessments, work at your own pace. Allow yourself time to reflect on your results and how they compare to what you already know about yourself.
- Do not answer the assessments as you think others would like you to answer them or how you think others see you. Remember that these assessments are for you to reflect on your life and explore some of the barriers that are keeping you from living a calmer, more rational and less anxious life.

Format of Book *(Continued)*

- Assessments are powerful tools if you are honest with yourself. Take your time and be truthful in your responses so that your results are an honest reflection of you. Your level of commitment in completing the assessments honestly will determine how much you learn about yourself.
- Before completing each assessment, be sure to read the instructions. The assessments have similar formats, but they have different scales, responses, scoring instructions and methods for interpretation.
- Finally, remember that learning about yourself should be a positive and motivating experience. Don't stress about taking the assessments or finding out about your results. Just respond honestly and learn as much about yourself as you can.

Guided Self-Exploration Activities

Guided self-exploration activities are any exercises that assist participants in self-reflection and enhance self-knowledge, identify potential ineffective behaviors, and teach more effective ways of coping. Guided self-exploration is designed to help participants make a series of discoveries that lead to increased social and emotional competencies, as well as to serve as an energizing way to help participants grow personally and professionally. They are brief, easy-to-use self-reflection tools designed to promote insight and self-growth. Many different types of guided self-exploration activities are provided for you to pick and chose the activities most needed by your participants and/or will be most appealing to them. The unique features of self-guided exploration activities make them usable and appropriate for a variety of individual sessions and group sessions.

Features of Guided Self-Exploration Activities

- **Quick, easy and rewarding to use** – These guided self-exploration activities are designed to be an efficient, appealing method for motivating participants to explore information about themselves - including their thoughts, feelings, and behaviors - in a relatively short period of time.
- **Reproducible** – Because the guided self-exploration activities can be reproduced by the facilitator, no more than the one book needs to be purchased. You may photocopy as many items as you wish for your participants. If you want to add or delete words on a page, make one photocopy, white out and/or write your own words, and then make photocopies from your personalized master.
- **Participative** – These guided self-exploration activities help people to quickly focus their attention, aid them in the self-reflection process, and learn new and more effective ways of coping.

Format of Book *(Continued)*

- **Motivating to complete** – The guided self-exploration activities are designed to be an energizing way for participants to engage in self-reflection and learn about themselves. Various activities are included to enhance the learning process related to developing important social and emotional competency skills.
- **Low risk** – The guided self-exploration activities are designed to be less risky than formal assessments and structured exercises. They are user-friendly, and participants will generally feel rewarded and motivated after completing these activities.
- **Adaptable to a variety of populations** – The guided self-exploration activities can be used with many different populations, and they can be tailored to meet the needs of the specific population with whom you work.
- **Focused** – Each guided self-exploration activity is designed to focus on a single coping issue, thus enhancing the experience for participants.
- **Flexible** – The guided self-exploration activities are flexible and can be used independently, or to supplement other types of interventions.

Chapter Elements

The Coping with Anxiety Workbook is designed to be used either independently or as part of an integrated curriculum. You may administer any of the assessments and the guided self-exploration activities to an individual or a group with whom you are working, or you may administer any of the activities over one or more days. Feel free to pick and choose those assessments and activities that best fit the outcomes you desire.

The first page of each chapter begins with an annotated Table of Contents with notes and examples for the facilitator.

Assessments – Assessments with scoring directions and interpretation materials begin each chapter. The authors recommend that you begin presenting each topic by asking participants to complete the assessment. Facilitators can choose one or more, or all of the activities relevant to their participants' specific needs and concerns.

Guided Self-Exploration Activities – Practical questions and activities to prompt self-reflection and promote self-understanding are included after each of the assessments. These questions and activities foster introspection and promote pro-social behaviors and coping skills. The activities in this workbook are tied to the assessments so that you can identify and select activities quickly and easily.

The activities are divided into four chapters to help you identify and select assessments easily and quickly:

Chapter 1: Anxiety Triggers
This chapter helps participants identify and learn to recognize their anxiety triggers.

Chapter 2: Fear Factor
This chapter helps participants identify and explore the intensity of their fears in life.

Chapter 3: Anxiety Symptoms
This chapter helps participants identify and explore how they experience symptoms of anxiety.

Chapter 4: Coping With My Anxiety
This chapter helps participants understand how effectively they are preventing and then coping with anxiety in life.

Thanks to . . .

Amy Brodsky, illustrator extraordinaire,
and to the following professionals whose input in this book has been invaluable!

Carol Butler, MS Ed, RN, C
Kathy Liptak, Ed.D.
Kathy Khalsa, MAJS, OTR/L
Eileen Regen, M.Ed., CJE
Jay Leutenberg

Table of Contents

ANXIETY TRIGGERS SCALE

FEAR FACTOR SCALE

Table of Contents *(continued)*

ANXIETY SYMPTOMS SCALE

COPING WITH MY ANXIETY SCALE

Anxiety Triggers

Table of Contents and Facilitator Notes

Explain to participants that triggers are environmental situations or events that initiate cognitions or emotions.

Distribute several copies to participants who have more characters to write about. Examples of characters might include George Castanza on Seinfeld, who is always worried that he has some rare disease, or Adrian Monk on Monk, who has anxieties and phobias about everything from milk to speaking in public.

Haiku is suggested, but participants do not need to focus on the haiku style. Participants can use any poem structure.

This activity is designed to help participants realize that often, what they believe to be the worst that can happen is not always that bad at all.

Bring a ball to the group and ask participants to imagine this being the crystal ball.

The list is not representative of all populations. Encourage participants to use the blank lines for the things they need to change.

Other Applicable Quotations

The key to change ... is to let go of fear. ~ Rosanne Cash

Nobody can go back and start a new beginning, but anyone can start today and make a new ending. ~ Maria Robinson

Sometimes it's the smallest decisions that can change your life forever. ~ Keri Russell

Table of Contents and Facilitator Notes

RELATIONSHIPS: *My son seems depressed and he will not seek help.*	*He won't get better and be able to live a fruitful life.*	*Talk to a friend of his to see if she can convince my son to find someone to talk with.*

Anxiety Triggers Scale Introduction

Anxiety is becoming an inevitable and increasingly prevalent part of our society.

As the pace of society increases, people must cope with changes in their social, environmental, corporate, and technological environments. It is important to realize that many situations in which it is appropriate to react anxiously arise in everyday life. However, some situations are not direct threats, but people still react anxiously.

The purpose of this assessment is to help you identify how much anxiety you are experiencing and what tends to trigger your anxiety. For each of the sections that follow, read each of the statements and decide if the statement applies to you always, sometimes or never. If it is *always* true for you, circle the number 3 next to the statement. If it is *sometimes* true for you, circle the number 2 next to the statement. If it is *never* true for you, circle the number 1, next to the statement. Complete all of the items before going back to score this scale.

In the following example, the circled 1 indicates that the item is never true for the participant completing the assessment:

	Always	Sometimes	Never
I get anxious when . . .			
I take a test	3	2	(1)

This is not a test and there are no right or wrong answers.
Do not spend too much time thinking about your answers.
Your initial response will be the most true for you.
Be sure to respond to every statement.

Name ____ **Date** ______________

Turn to the next page and begin.

Scale: Anxiety Triggers

	Always	Sometimes	Never
I get anxious when . . .			
I take a test	3	2	1
I find myself in an uncomfortable conversation	3	2	1
I interview for a job	3	2	1
I go to a party or social event	3	2	1
I meet a new person	3	2	1
I go on a date or have a meeting with someone new	3	2	1
I am around children	3	2	1
I talk on the phone to a customer service representative	3	2	1
I go to the store	3	2	1
I am about to be evaluated at work	3	2	1
I have to speak or perform in public	3	2	1
I go to the dentist or doctor	3	2	1
I am surrounded by prejudiced people	3	2	1
I am going to be late	3	2	1
I am unable to do something perfectly	3	2	1

A - TOTAL = ____________

(Continued on the next page)

Scale: Anxiety Triggers *(Continued)*

I get anxious when I think about . . .	Always	Sometimes	Never
caring for an aging family member	3	2	1
being downsized or fired from my job	3	2	1
keeping up with current technology	3	2	1
something different happening at work	3	2	1
a change in my family situation	3	2	1
a personal health issue	3	2	1
problems with members of my family	3	2	1
moving from my residence to another	3	2	1
new thoughts about my religion or spiritual beliefs	3	2	1
beginning or finishing an education training program	3	2	1
financial issues	3	2	1
the health problem of a family member	3	2	1
my marital status	3	2	1
future retirement plans	3	2	1
my relationship issues	3	2	1

C - TOTAL = ____________

(Continued on the next page)

Scale: Anxiety Triggers *(Continued)*

When I worry . . .	Always	Sometimes	Never
I have irrational thoughts	3	2	1
I avoid the situation or object I fear	3	2	1
I feel powerless	3	2	1
I have trouble relaxing	3	2	1
it is usually about small, insignificant things	3	2	1
it is often about things I have no control over	3	2	1
it gets in my way at work	3	2	1
I can't function effectively	3	2	1
it influences my dreams	3	2	1
it affects my sleep	3	2	1
it becomes so intense I feel panicky	3	2	1
it interferes with my normal routine	3	2	1
it creates problems for me at work	3	2	1
it affects my relationships	3	2	1
it creates stress and anxiety for me	3	2	1

W - TOTAL = ____________

GO TO THE SCORING DIRECTIONS

Anxiety Triggers Scale
Scoring Directions

The Anxiety Triggers Scale is designed to help you to identify the primary triggers for your feelings of anxiety.

Scoring the Anxiety Triggers Scale:

Look at the items you just completed. Add the numbers you've circled for each of the three sections (A, C, and W) on the previous pages. Put that total on the line marked TOTAL at the end of each section.

Transfer your totals for each of the three sections to the lines below:

SCALE A: Anxieties Total = ________

SCALE C: Changes Total = ________

SCALE W: Worries Total = ________

The Profile Interpretation section that follows will help you understand your scores.

Profile Interpretation

Individual Scale Score	Result	Indications
15 to 24	low	If you scored in the Low range on any of the scales, you do not experience very much anxiety due to these anxiety-producing situations or objects.
25 to 35	moderate	If you scored in the Moderate range on any of the scales, you experience some anxiety due to these anxiety-producing situations or objects.
36 to 45	high	If you scored in the High range on any of the scales, you experience a great deal of anxiety due to these anxiety-producing situations or objects.

What Triggers Your Anxiety?

**We all become anxious about different situations.
What triggers your anxiety?**

1) Increases in physical or mental stress

❑ Changes at work	❑ Other ____________
❑ Completing an educational goal	❑ Other ____________
❑ Changes in finances	❑ Other ____________
❑ Change in personal health	❑ Other ____________
❑ Change in health of someone close	❑ Other ____________

2) Relationship Issues

❑ Divorce / Separation / Split up	❑ Other ____________
❑ Marriage	❑ Other ____________
❑ Arguments	❑ Other ____________
❑ Family, in-laws	❑ Other ____________
❑ Friends and neighbors	❑ Other ____________

3) Anxiety-provoking events

❑ Death of someone close	❑ Other ____________
❑ Poor performance	❑ Other ____________
❑ Personal injury / Poor health	❑ Other ____________
❑ Retirement	❑ Other ____________
❑ Pregnancy	❑ Other ____________
❑ Financial problems	❑ Other ____________
❑ Speaking in public	❑ Other ____________
❑ Loss of a job	❑ Other ____________

Being aware of what triggers our anxieties is the first step in managing them.

Movie and/or Television Characters

Think about two of your favorite movie or television characters. Do any of them have anxieties? What are they? How do they deal with them?

Movie or Television Character ____________________

What movie or television show?____________________

What are his or her anxieties?____________________

____

____

How does this character deal with these anxieties?____________________

____

____

Do you think they managed their anxiety effectively or ineffectively? Why?

____

____

Movie or Television Character ____________________

What movie or television show?____________________

What are his or her anxieties?____________________

____

____

How does this character deal with these anxieties?____________________

____

____

Do you think they managed their anxiety effectively or ineffectively? Why?

____

____

Anxiety Poetry

A haiku is a short poem using three lines to convey one thought. No rhyme is required in this type of poem.

For example:

Thoughts going wild
anxiety at its worst
need to get control

Think about how you feel when you are anxious, or something about which you are anxious, and create your own haiku (or any other style) poem.

What's The Worst That Could Happen?

Think about a time when you felt anxious. What was the situation?

How did you feel internally?

What was the worst thing that could have happened in that situation?

What did happen?

In the future, can you go through the same situation with less anxiety?

The Crystal Ball

People who experience anxiety often make negative predictions about their future, and these predictions often become self-fulfilling prophesies. Anxiety can be likened to looking at the future through a crystal ball. It is important that you examine your negative predictions. The following exercise will help you examine the anticipatory anxiety in your life.

Explain something that happened in your past about which you were anxious.

____

____

Why did you feel anxious about this?

____

____

What did you fear would happen?

____

____

How did you think you would feel in the situation?

____

____

How did you actually feel in the situation?

____

____

Did what you were worried about actually happen?

____

____

How did your thinking affect the anxiety you felt?

____

____

How will you react in the future when you face a similar situation?

____

____

I Want to Make a Change

It is healthy and healing to decide to make beneficial changes which will alleviate anxiety in your own life.

Place a check in the box by those you would like to improve and/or change.

- ❑ My relationships or marriage
- ❑ The health care of a loved one
- ❑ My education
- ❑ My negative thinking
- ❑ My caregiver status
- ❑ My ability to ask for help
- ❑ My self-esteem
- ❑ My patience level
- ❑ My computer skills
- ❑ Learn to say "no" when I want to
- ❑ Make new friends
- ❑ ______________________
- ❑ ______________________
- ❑ ______________________
- ❑ ______________________
- ❑ ______________________

- ❑ My retirement dreams
- ❑ My work situation
- ❑ The place where I live
- ❑ My financial situation
- ❑ My social life
- ❑ My physical fitness
- ❑ Try to express my feelings
- ❑ Become more responsible
- ❑ Set boundaries
- ❑ Find time to volunteer
- ❑ Manage my anger and frustration
- ❑ ______________________
- ❑ ______________________
- ❑ ______________________
- ❑ ______________________
- ❑ ______________________

Circle one item from the 1st column that is important to you.
How would you benefit by making this change?

____

____

____

Now, circle one item from the 2nd column that is important to you.
How would you benefit by making this change?

____

____

____

A Change in My Life

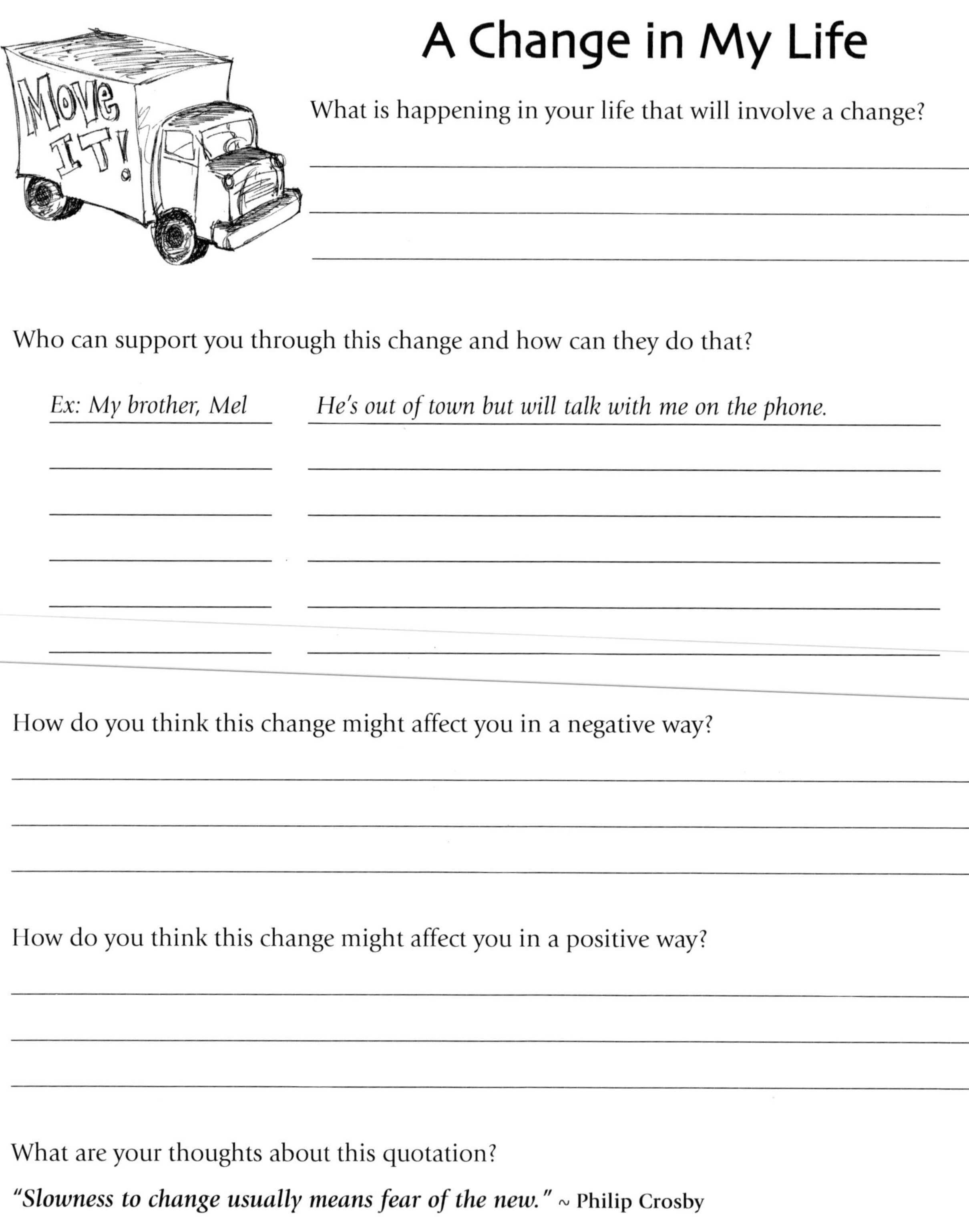

What is happening in your life that will involve a change?

____

____

____

Who can support you through this change and how can they do that?

Ex: My brother, Mel	*He's out of town but will talk with me on the phone.*

How do you think this change might affect you in a negative way?

____

____

____

How do you think this change might affect you in a positive way?

____

____

____

What are your thoughts about this quotation?

"Slowness to change usually means fear of the new." ~ **Philip Crosby**

____

____

____

Making Changes

Making a change is a process.
Carefully thinking out the change will be valuable.

1) A **CHANGE** might need to be made

What do you want to change?

____

____

____

2) A **DECISION** might need to be made

What might your decision be?

____

____

____

3) Time to develop a **PLAN OF ACTION**

What might your plan of action be?

Step 1. ______________________________

____

____

Step 2. ______________________________

____

____

Step 3. ______________________________

____

____

Step 4. ______________________________

____

____

The Serenity Prayer

The Serenity Prayer helps us recognize and think about the differences between the things we cannot change (what we have no control over) and the things we can change (what we do have control over).

(On the blank lines, write the things that come to your mind.)

Grant me the serenity to

Accept the things I cannot change . . .

Courage to change the things I can . . .

And the wisdom to know the difference.

My CHANGE Cartoon Strip

Everyone likes cartoons! Cartoons can be very much like real life.

Ex: What I thought would happen

Ex: What actually happened

Think about a situation in the past when you had a huge change in your life.

Draw what you *thought* would happen.

Now, draw what *actually* happened.

Were there differences? What were they?____

____

____

____

Today's Worry

**Excessive worrying takes an emotional toll on us.
It is important to evaluate our worries, their importance, and whether we have control over the worry.**

Let's evaluate one of your worries. What is one of your worries today?

____

____

Circle whether it's *extremely / very / somewhat / just a little* worrisome to you.

What kind of control do you have over this?

What can you do?

____

____

____

How can you gain control of it?

____

____

____

If you have no control, how can you let go?

____

____

____

What can you say to yourself when you find yourself worrying about this again?

____

____

____

____

Situations I Usually Worry About

Identify five situations that you tend to worry about.
These situations could occur at home, work, during your leisure time, in relationships, your community or the global community.

	My worry	What can I do about it?
1) HOME		
2) WORK		
3) LEISURE TIME		
4) RELATIONSHIPS		
5) COMMUNITY		
OTHER		

The Worry Pie

Name one of your worries. ______________________________

Shade or color in the times you feel you worry about the above situation. If you worry in your sleep or dream about it, count that time also.

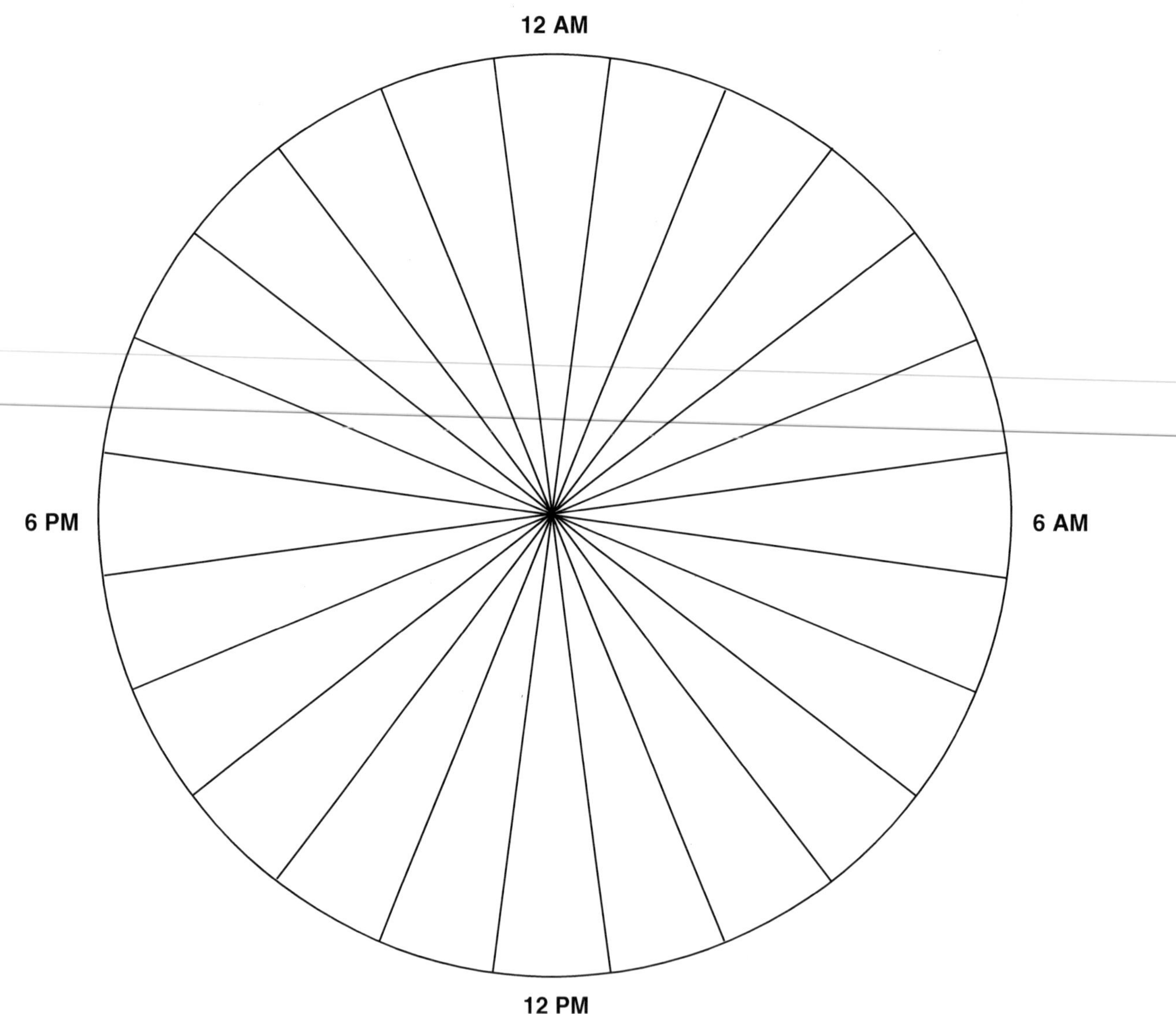

Make a commitment to worry about this________ minutes a day, and then, LET IT GO!

Doodling

Doodling is an excellent way for you to unleash the power of self-expression. You do not need to be an artist to doodle. You are the only one who needs to know what the doodle represents. Doodling is simply drawing something without thinking a lot about it. It is designed to help you put your left logical brain on hold while you use your right creative brain. Doodles can be silly designs, drawings, abstract shapes, or simply lines.

My greatest worry is …	When I worry, I feel …
When I worry, my stomach feels like …	When I worry, the thoughts going through my mind feel like …

Letting Go of My Worries

Having the ability to let go of your worries, even if you worry for 15 minutes and then let go of them for the rest of the day, is an important, healthy coping skill.

In the kites below, write three of your worries, and visualize yourself holding the kites and then letting them go, one by one. Watch each one go up higher and higher, getting smaller and smaller, until you can no longer see, or worry about them.

Fear Factor

Table of Contents and Facilitator Notes

Fear is a normal human emotion brought on by a perceived actual threat. Phobias are irrational, strong fears and avoidance of one particular object (e.g., spiders) or situation (riding on an elevator). Fears have a limited basis in reality.

After participants complete the handout, ask for volunteers to make some of the emotions faces and other participants can guess the emotion.

Ex: Jill gets anxious when she has to talk in front of large groups of people. Therefore, before she begins she closes her eyes, takes three deep breaths, and eliminates all of the internal chatter taking place in her head. Then she is ready to talk to large groups.

Distribute extra sheets of blank papers for participants to create doodles and caricatures.

MY AGE	WHAT I BECAME AFRAID OF	WHAT HAPPENED?
11 - 20	EX: Swimming	At 16 years old I almost drowned

Facilitator can bring some examples, i.e., funny calendar, cute DVD, comic book, jokes, etc.

Ask for volunteers to read their letters to their fears.

Ex: Your Fear: Elevators

Ex: Your Fear's Talk: "Why are you worried about me? The ride will be short and the door will open when you reach your destination. I am inspected regularly."

Table of Contents and Facilitator Notes

Ex: Support network O → 7 5 ← *(5 = just right)*
Positive Attitude O 6
Fear is under control O 7

Ex: My greatest fear is: speaking in public
I am afraid because: People will be watching me
People will comment negatively on my performance

Suggest that participants cut out the coping affirmations and post in strategic places (by computer, on a mirror, or keep them in a pocket or wallet, etc.)

Cut out the strips of paper, then fold and place them in a container. One-by-one, ask each person to pick one and demonstrate that body language. The other participants can discuss what they think the body language characteristics represent.

Interpretations: *Hand on cheek = Thinking or evaluating ...*
Standing hands behind back = Confident ...
Constantly patting or fixing hair = Not confident ...
Lowered head = Acceptance of defeat ...
Clearing throat often = Anxious ...
Chin up and towards another person = Aggressive ....
Tug an ear = Indecisive ...
Tilting Head = Interested ...
Lack of eye-contact = Lack of self confidence ...
Lowering eyes = Submission, fear or guilt ...
Folded or crossed arms = Not happy about what is being said or done ...
Walking briskly and upright posture = Confidence ...
Fiddling with items = Boredom or anxious ...
Looking upward and to the right = Recalling a memory ...
Crossing ankles, legs stretched = Relaxed ...
Tapping or drumming fingers = Impatience or frustration ...

Ask participants if they have friends who are very shy. Talk about how shyness affects their relationship.

Support Person	Why I Chose This Person	When is this Person Available?	Phone
Ex: Mom	She understands that I have always had a fear of heights.	Anytime	000-0000

Ask participants to keep their completed notes in a strategic spot and refer to them after a week, month and year.

Fear Factor Scale Introduction

All people have developed and maintained certain fears throughout their lives. These fears can be common things such as being afraid of snakes, and may not interfere with relationships, work and daily living habits. On the other hand, these fears can be intense and significantly interfere with how you live your life. The Fear Factor Scale can help you identify and explore how intense the fears in your life are.

The assessment contains 22 statements. With TRUE or FALSE as your choice, read each of the statements and circle TRUE if the statement applies to you or circle FALSE if it doesn't.

When it comes to fears . . .

I am not afraid of too many things **TRUE** **(FALSE)**

In the above statement, the circled FALSE means that the statement does not describe the test taker.

This is not a test and there are no right or wrong answers. Do not spend too much time thinking about your answers. Your initial response will be the most true for you.
Be sure to respond to every statement.

Name ______________________________ **Date** ______________

Turn to the next page and begin.

Scale: Fear Factor

When it comes to my fears . . .

I do not have many phobias (irrational, intense and persistent fears) . . . . TRUE FALSE

I don't let my fears hold me back. . . . . TRUE FALSE

I have some techniques for dealing with my fears . . . . TRUE FALSE

I tend to be rational about my fears. . . . . TRUE FALSE

My fears do not interfere with my daily activities. . . . . TRUE FALSE

I don't try to avoid the situations I fear . . . . TRUE FALSE

I rarely feel powerless because of my fears . . . . TRUE FALSE

I am able to relax despite my fears or phobias . . . . TRUE FALSE

My fears do not interfere with my performance on my job . . . . TRUE FALSE

I do not panic when I encounter one of my fears or phobias . . . . TRUE FALSE

I have supportive people in my life who help me face my fears . . . . TRUE FALSE

I do not have many fears . . . . TRUE FALSE

My fears are usually rational and real . . . . TRUE FALSE

I have no trouble relaxing despite my fears or phobias . . . . TRUE FALSE

I picture helpful imagery when I think about my fears . . . . TRUE FALSE

My fears are not debilitating. . . . . TRUE FALSE

My fears do not hinder my career achievements. . . . . TRUE FALSE

I will not avoid an object or situation that I fear . . . . TRUE FALSE

Exposure to my fears do not cause me to panic . . . . TRUE FALSE

My fears do not interfere with my relationships. . . . . TRUE FALSE

I manage the stress associated with my fears. . . . . TRUE FALSE

I face my fears when it's necessary . . . . TRUE FALSE

TOTAL = ___________

GO TO THE SCORING DIRECTIONS

Fear Factor Scale Scoring Directions

It is critical to begin to learn about and understand the effect hat your fears are having on your life, career, and relationships. The Fear Factor Scale is designed to measure the level of intensity that your fears play in your daily functioning.

Scoring the Fear Factor Scale:

For each of the items you completed, count the TRUE words that you circled. Put that total on the line marked TOTAL at the end of the section.

Then, transfer your totals to the space below:

FEAR FACTOR TOTAL = __________

Profile Interpretation

Individual Scale Score	Result	Indications
0 to 7	low	If you scored in the Low range on the scale, you are experiencing a great deal of anxiety due to your fears and phobias.
8 to 14	moderate	If you scored in the Moderate range on the scale, you are experiencing some anxiety due to your fears and phobias.
15 to 22	high	If you scored in the High range on the scale, you are not experiencing a lot of anxiety due to your fears and phobias.

No matter how you scored, low, moderate or high, you will benefit from these exercises.

Fears Affecting My Life

Which of these fears affect your daily living?

- ❑ abuse
- ❑ aging
- ❑ airplanes
- ❑ being alone
- ❑ bridges
- ❑ closed in spaces
- ❑ clowns
- ❑ contagious illness
- ❑ crowds
- ❑ darkness
- ❑ dentists
- ❑ doctors
- ❑ dogs
- ❑ driving
- ❑ drowning
- ❑ dying
- ❑ elevators
- ❑ escalators
- ❑ germs
- ❑ heights
- ❑ hospitals
- ❑ insects
- ❑ leaving the house
- ❑ lightning
- ❑ malls
- ❑ needles
- ❑ open spaces
- ❑ parents aging
- ❑ public speaking
- ❑ roller coasters
- ❑ sight of blood
- ❑ snakes
- ❑ social situations
- ❑ spiders
- ❑ thunderstorms
- ❑ trains
- ❑ water
- ❑ ____________
- ❑ ____________
- ❑ ____________
- ❑ ____________
- ❑ ____________
- ❑ ____________
- ❑ ____________
- ❑ ____________

Which of these fears affect your daily living?

____

____

What are some negative consequences of your fears?

____

____

____

What have you done to overcome your fears?

____

____

____

What can you now do to overcome your fears?

____

____

____

Emotions Connected to My Fears

Place a checkmark by the faces
that represent how you feel when you are fearful.

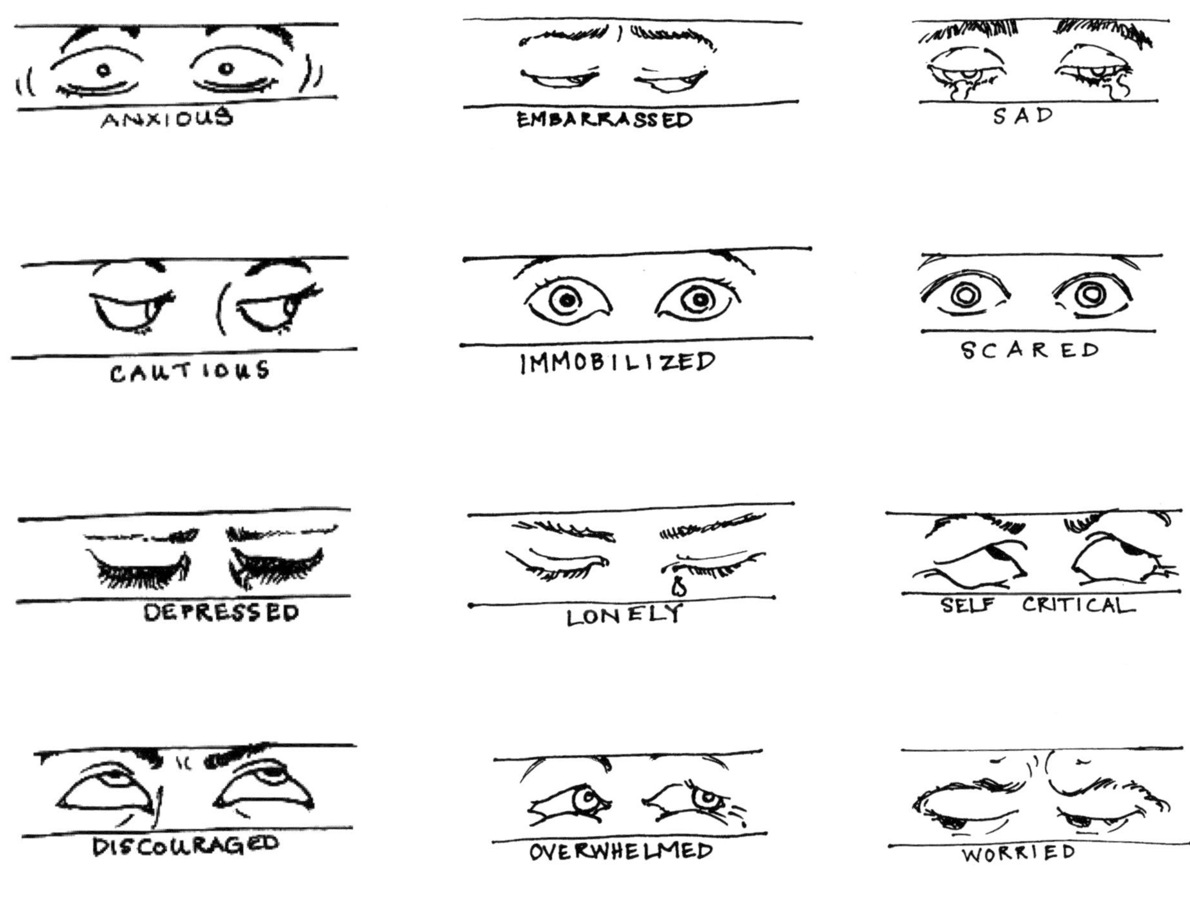

When you are emotional in a fearful situation, you have choices. You can . . .

- ❑ Talk with a supportive person
- ❑ Get a hug
- ❑ Have a good cry and go forward
- ❑ Take deep breaths
- ❑ Go for a walk
- ❑ Browse at a bookstore
- ❑ Take a drive
- ❑ Play with a pet
- ❑ Meditate
- ❑ Enjoy some quiet-time
- ❑ ______________________
- ❑ ______________________
- ❑ ______________________
- ❑ ______________________
- ❑ ______________________
- ❑ ______________________

Fear Coping Strategies

Fear can immobilize you, especially during a time of uncertainty and when you face circumstances beyond your control. Check off the fear coping strategies that you are willing to try.

__ Remember that some fear is normal
__ Rehearse your fear situation
__ Tolerate your feelings of fear
__ Say "I can do it!"
__ Keep a positive attitude
__ Reach out to a supportive friend
__ Be proud of small steps
__ Give yourself a reward for each step
__ Forget failed attempts
__ Take deep breaths
__ Keep inspiring quotes nearby
__ Remember you don't need to be perfect
__ Meditate
__ Express yourself
__ Do not minimize or exaggerate issues
__ Keep your sense of humor
__ Use positive self-talk
__ Talk to someone who listens well
__ Seek spiritual support
__ Take care of your body

List three of the coping skills above that you are willing to try and give examples of how you might do that:

1) ____

____

____

____

2) ____

____

____

____

3) ____

____

____

____

Caricatures

Caricatures are exaggerated or distorted likenesses. You don't need to be an artist to draw caricatures. They just need to make sense to you, to depict what your fears look like in your mind.

Example: Fear of an elevator

Draw a caricature of one of your fears.

Early Fear Memories

Often, fears are results of something that happened in the past. What are the earliest memories you have of anxiety-producing fears?

MY AGE	WHAT I BECAME AFRAID OF	WHAT HAPPENED?
0 - 10		
11 - 20		
21 - 30		
31 - 40		
41 - 50		
51 - 60		
61 +		

CONSIDER THIS:

It may be in your power to refuse to allow these past memories to influence your life!

Lighten Up

Laughter is the best medicine for healing and for fear. It takes the energy out of the fear, lifts your spirits and helps you to relax and enjoy.

Check the lighten-up situations that appeal to you.

Brighten up someone else's day. . . . . ____
Enjoy a funny 365-day calendar by looking at it every day . . . . ____
Face your own imperfections with laughter . . . . ____
Have crayons or color pencils and paper available . . . . ____
Keep a colorful, fun jig-saw puzzle on a table . . . . ____
Laugh at yourself . . . . ____
Place fun toys in a handy drawer to keep the environment playful . . . . . . ____
Play board games . . . . ____
Find a fun shop and purchase a gift for someone you care about . . . . ____
Recall funny moments of the past and record them in a journal . . . . ____
Set up a bulletin board at home or work for cartoons and jokes . . . . ____
Sing and/or dance . . . . ____
Smile a lot! . . . . ____
Spend time with positive people who do not drain your energy . . . . ____
Stock your shelves with humorous books . . . . ____
Take time with friends who are supportive and laugh easily. . . . . ____
Tape and/or watch television comedy shows . . . . ____
Use fun mugs, T-shirts, buttons and posters . . . . ____
Watch movies that are light and fun . . . . ____
Write jokes on paper when you hear them and pass them along . . . . ____

Put a * by your top 3. Write how you will use those lighten-up situations.

1) ____

____

2) ____

____

3) ____

____

Talk To Your Fear

Write a letter to one of your fears describing your feelings about this fear and how much time you devote to worrying about it.
Describe how this fear affects your life and the lives of those around you.
Describe what you will do to stop being afraid of this situation.

You, ____

____, are my fear.

My feelings about you are______________________________

____

____.

I spend ______________time worrying about you because ______________

____

____

____.

This affects my life ______________________________

____

____

____.

It also affects those around me by______________________

____

____

____.

This is what I am going to do about my fear of you ______________

____

____

____

____

____.

My Fear Talks Back

Write a short dialogue from the standpoint of your fears. If your fears could talk, what could they say to alleviate your anxiety? Now you try.

YOUR FEAR – ______________________________

____

____

YOUR FEAR TALKS BACK – "______________________________

____

______________________________"

YOUR FEAR – ______________________________

____

____

YOUR FEAR TALKS BACK – "______________________________

____

______________________________"

YOUR FEAR – ______________________________

____

____

YOUR FEAR TALKS BACK – "______________________________

____

______________________________"

Healthy Lifestyle

It is imperative to cultivate a healthy lifestyle as an important tool in managing stress and keeping fears under control. Determine your healthy lifestyle by placing an arrow from the circle by each item to the number that rates how much you currently incorporated this lifestyle factor in your life.

Sleep **O**	1	← (1 = too little)
Stress management **O**	2	
Significant/family relationships **O**	3	
Socialize **O**	4	
Support network **O**	5	← (5 = just right)
Positive attitude **O**	6	
Fear is under control **O**	7	
Exercise **O**	8	
Nutrition **O**	9	
Regular medical check-ups **O**	10	← (10 = too much)

What do you need to do to get as close to a number 5 in each of the items that you rated 1, 2, 3, 7, 8, 9 or 10?

1) ______________________________

2) ______________________________

3) ______________________________

7) ______________________________

8) ______________________________

9) ______________________________

10) ______________________________

Fear Factor

What is your greatest fear and what are the reasons you are afraid?

My greatest fear is ______________________________

____

____

____

I am afraid because ______________________________

____

____

____

____

____

____

____

____

____

Do you believe your fear rational? ❑ YES ❑ NO

Do you believe your fear realistic? ❑ YES ❑ NO

What can you do to face this fear?

____

____

____

____

____

____

____

Preparing to Face a Fear

Facing your fears can be an intense experience. When facing a fear, you can better prepare yourself by using coping statements.

Today I am going to face my fear of __________________________________.

This is the best way to overcome this fear.

I am going to go a little bit out of my comfort zone to face my fear.

This is my way of becoming more comfortable with this fear.

I will continue to take small steps to overcome my fear.

I will learn to live with less anxiety in my life.

Here are some affirmations to help you cope.

I will take small steps.
I have managed this situation before, and I can do it again.
I will relax and go slowly.
I will know I did my very best and I will be okay.
This is just another adventure in my life.
I can handle the sensations that accompany this fear.
This is just adrenaline – it will pass soon.
I'm just experiencing anxiety and it will pass.
I don't need to be perfect.
I can do it!

Look Confident ⇨ Feel Confident

One of the ways people form opinions about others is by observing their body language. Body language is non-verbal communication through the use of postures, gestures and facial expressions. Using confident body language helps us to feel confident. Place a C in each of box that shows confidence. Place an A in each box that shows anxiety.

Standing hands behind back	Folded or crossed arms
Hand on cheek	Walking briskly and upright posture
Tug an ear	Fiddling with items
Constantly patting or fixing hair	Looking upward and to the right
Lowered head	Lowering eyes
Clearing throat often	Lack of eye-contact
Chin up and towards another person	Tilting Head
Crossing ankles, legs stretched	Tapping or drumming fingers

On the reverse side of this page, draw a picture of yourself in an upcoming situation, using the confident body language.

Later, practice the positive gestures in front of the group, a friend, or in the mirror.

Shyness and Social Fears

People who are very shy or have fear of other people may have a persistent and irrational fear of social or performance situations. They often feel socially awkward and might avoid these situations entirely.

Which of these types of thinking come to mind when you are faced with a social situation?

- ❑ People will laugh at me
- ❑ I won't know what to say
- ❑ People will think I am silly
- ❑ People will not like what I have to say
- ❑ I will appear to be stupid or incompetent
- ❑ I will look ridiculous

SUGGESTIONS FOR RETHINKING YOUR FEARS

- ✓ Consider whether you have actual evidence of your fearful thinking
- ✓ Use realistic self-talk ("I can do this." "I will be fine." "I am okay.")
- ✓ Count your breaths until the fearful thinking disappears
- ✓ Visualize yourself being successful in the situation
- ✓ Remember, even if you were not successful previously in the same type of situation, you can be now!

What is an upcoming social situation which concerns you?

____

____

How will you use the suggestions above to help reduce your social fears?

____

____

____

My FEAR Support System

There are different ways of managing a fear. Whether you choose to confront the fear or live with it, it is important to have a support system. This means having an individual or group of people that you trust to help you through the process. Your support system offers kind words of support, and understanding and encouragement to go out and meet your fear. Your support system can include family, friends, co-workers and anyone you know who has your best interest at heart.

Complete the following chart and keep it available to remind you of who to contact when needed.

SUPPORT PERSON	WHY I CHOSE THIS PERSON	WHEN IS THIS PERSON AVAILABLE	PHONE

My Fear Goal

Goal setting is one way to begin moving in a positive direction.

Your goal must be reasonable and measurable.

ONE OF MY BIGGEST FEARS:

____

____

MY GOALS IN FACING THIS FEAR:

In the **next week** I will ____

____

____

____

____

In the **next month** I will ____

____

____

____

____

Within the **year** I will ____

____

____

____

____

Signed ______________________________ **Date** ____________________

Anxiety Symptoms

Table of Contents and Facilitator Notes

Take a poll of the participants' answers and discuss where the group feels anxiety on their body.

MY ANXIETY - PRODUCING SITUATION	THE THOUGHTS THAT GO THROUGH MY HEAD	HOW I FEEL WHEN THIS SITUATION HAPPENS
Mother is at home alone and isn't well.	*She might fall or be unable to take her medications.*	*Scared, anxious, heart pounding, unable to focus.*

If able, bring some healthy snacks as a treat and good example.

After participants complete the handout, ask if they would be willing to share what they ate yesterday that is on their list and examples of what they listed as possible substitute.

Ask if anyone would be willing to share what they wrote at the bottom of the page.

WHAT HAPPENED?	HOW DID I FEEL?	HOW LONG DID MY FEELINGS LAST?
My work supervisor told me that people may have to be laid off.	*Scared, angry and surprised*	*Several days*

Table of Contents and Facilitator Notes

Anxiety Symptoms Introduction

Everyone experiences anxiety, but we all react to anxiety very differently. Some people experience physical symptoms like shortness of breath and feeling cold. On the other hand, some people experience the symptoms of anxiety in an emotional way like feeling lonely or bored.

This assessment contains descriptors of the symptoms of anxiety and is divided into two sections. Think about the times when you were feeling anxious. Place a check in the boxes that describe your reactions to the anxiety. In the following example, the ☑ shows that the person completing the assessment has chills and a clenched jaw when experiencing anxieties.

When I am anxious, I experience…

- ❑ Back pain
- ☑ Chills
- ☑ Clenched jaw
- ❑ Cold, clammy hands

This is not a test and there are no right or wrong answers. Do not spend too much time thinking about your answers. Your initial response will be the most true for you. Be sure to respond to every statement.

Name ______________________________ **Date** ______________

Turn to the next page and begin.

Scale: Anxiety Symptoms

When I am anxious, I experience…

- ❑ Back pain
- ❑ Chills
- ❑ Clenched jaw
- ❑ Cold, clammy hands
- ❑ Constant colds
- ❑ Constipation
- ❑ Diarrhea
- ❑ Eating disorder
- ❑ Dizziness
- ❑ Finger tapping
- ❑ Grinding teeth
- ❑ Hand wringing
- ❑ Headaches
- ❑ Heaviness in my chest
- ❑ High blood pressure
- ❑ Hot flashes
- ❑ Inability to cope
- ❑ Inability to eat
- ❑ Jittery
- ❑ Lack of energy
- ❑ Lightheaded
- ❑ Neck pain
- ❑ Nervous energy
- ❑ Overeating
- ❑ Pacing
- ❑ Pressured speech
- ❑ Profuse sweating
- ❑ Rapid heartbeat
- ❑ Restless sleep
- ❑ Shaking all over
- ❑ Shaking knees
- ❑ Shortness of breath
- ❑ Skin rash
- ❑ Sleepless nights
- ❑ Tight muscles
- ❑ Trembling
- ❑ Upset stomach
- ❑ Use of addictive substances

P TOTAL = __________

GO TO THE NEXT PAGE

Scale: Anxiety Symptoms *(continued)*

When I am anxious, I feel…

- ❑ Aggressive
- ❑ Alienated
- ❑ Angry
- ❑ Annoyed
- ❑ Apathetic
- ❑ Apprehensive
- ❑ Bored
- ❑ Cautious
- ❑ Confused
- ❑ Depressed
- ❑ Disconnected
- ❑ Distracted
- ❑ Edgy
- ❑ Exhausted
- ❑ Fearful
- ❑ Forgetful
- ❑ Frustrated
- ❑ Gloomy
- ❑ Guilty
- ❑ Helpless
- ❑ Hyperactive
- ❑ Impulsive
- ❑ Irrational
- ❑ Irritable
- ❑ Isolated
- ❑ Lonely
- ❑ Miserable
- ❑ Moody
- ❑ Obsessive
- ❑ Overwhelmed
- ❑ Panicky
- ❑ Pessimistic
- ❑ Regretful
- ❑ Restless
- ❑ Sad
- ❑ Tearful
- ❑ Withdrawn
- ❑ Worrisome

E TOTAL = ______________

GO TO THE SCORING DIRECTIONS

Anxiety Symptoms Scale
Scoring Directions

Everyone experiences symptoms of anxiety.
It is important to identify your symptoms when you are anxious,
become aware of them and notice how this affects you.

Scoring the Anxiety Symptoms Scale:

This assessment will help you explore the various ways you experience symptoms of anxiety. For each of the sections, count the number of boxes in which you placed a ✓. Your score will range from 0 to 38. Put that total on the line marked TOTAL at the end of each section.

Transfer your totals to the spaces below:

P (PHYSICAL) TOTAL = ________

E (EMOTIONAL) TOTAL = ________

Profile Interpretation

Individual Scales Score	Result	Indications
26 to 38	high	If you score high on either of the scales, you tend to experience a great deal of anxiety.
13 to 25	moderate	If you score moderate on either of the scales, you tend to experience some anxiety.
0 to 12	low	If you score low on either of the scales, you tend to not experience much anxiety.

No matter how you scored, low, moderate or high, you will benefit from these exercises.

Tuning Into Your Body

THE PROCESS

To effectively access your feelings, you need to shift the focus from your **head** to your **body**. To do so, try the following exercise:

Physically relax using mindfulness or meditation.

Ask yourself, "What am I feeling right now?"

Identify where in your body you are feeling the feeling(s).

Tune into the feeling(s) to learn all you can.

Ask yourself, "What is my main concern or problem?"

Now you try it! Think about something you are worried about in the future.

Physically relax using mindfulness or meditation. Mindfulness is being in the present, and becoming more aware of your thoughts, feelings, actions, and surroundings. In mindfulness you lower the noise in your environment, bring your attention to the present moment, and let all things fall away. You can practice focusing on your breath or any other object so that your mind becomes quite clear. When you catch your mind wandering onto other topics, you calmly bring your attention back to your breathing. Slowly counting your breaths may help your concentration. Do not allow your anxieties to break through your concentration.

Ask yourself, "What am I feeling right now?"

Identify where in your body you are feeling the feeling(s).

Tune into the feeling(s) to learn all you can.

Ask yourself, "What is my main concern or problem?"

You Try it!

Symptom-Mapping

Symptom-mapping is a very effective method for better understanding your anxieties and the effect that they have in your life. For the following symptom map, start in the center. In the middle circle, list one of the anxieties you have today. Then next to the other circles, list how that fear affects different aspects of your life.

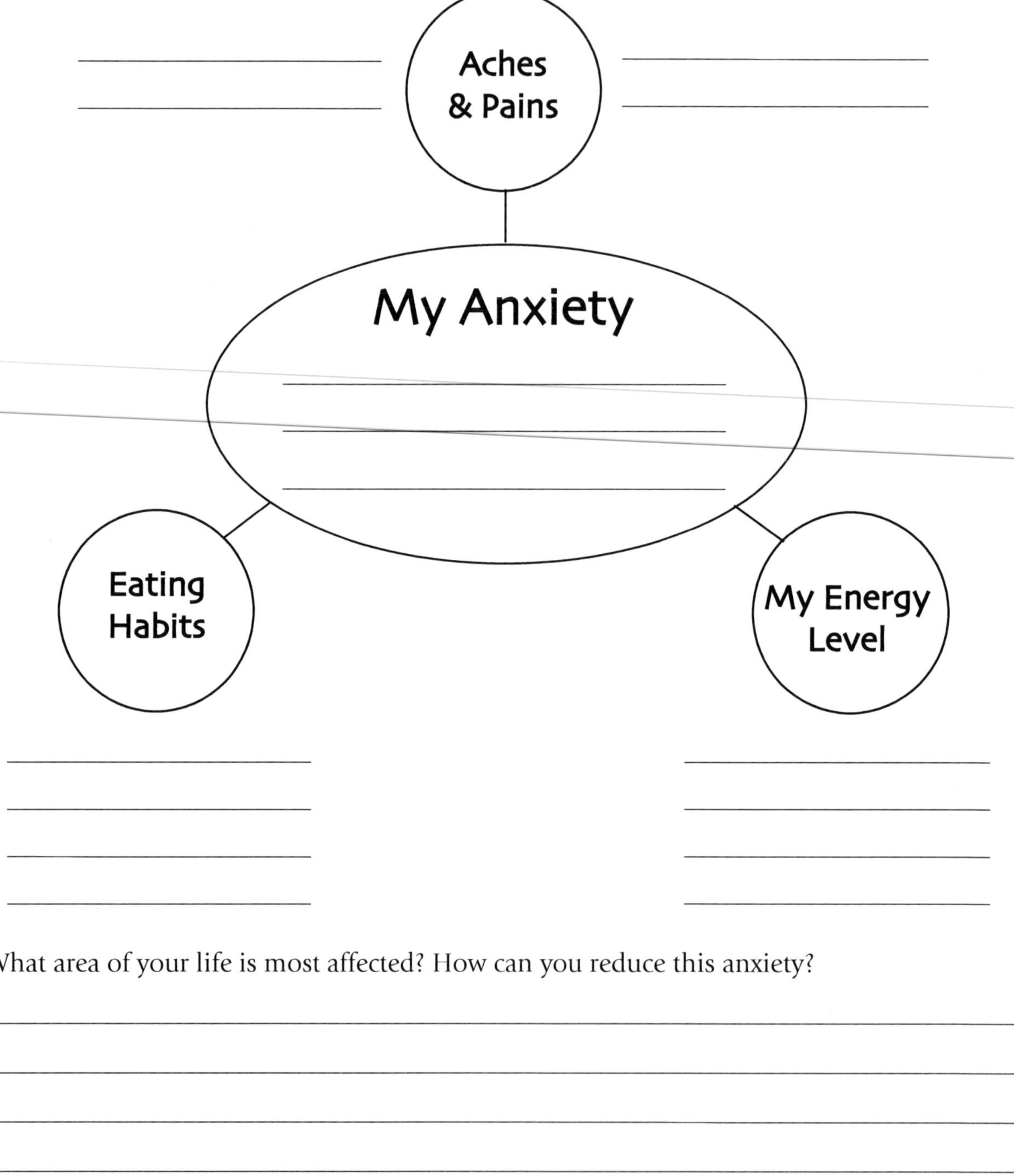

What area of your life is most affected? How can you reduce this anxiety?

Physical Symptoms

You probably feel tension in your body when you hold in your feelings of anxiety. For example, you may experience anger and frustration in your upper back and neck, while fear may be experienced in the pit of your stomach. On the picture below, identify and write on the drawing the feelings you suppress and where you feel them on your body.

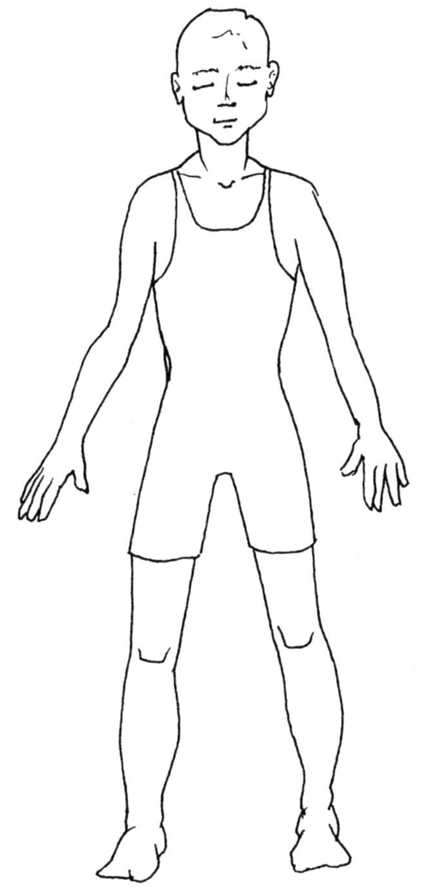

Where on your body do you tend to feel anxiety the most?

____

____

How do you most effectively deal with these physical symptoms?

____

____

What things could you do to prevent anxiety from affecting your body so much?

____

____

Anxiety Feelings from Thoughts

Feelings are influenced by your thoughts and perceptions. They often arise when you interpret events and react to your own internal self-talk.

Complete the table below. In the future, when you feel yourself becoming anxious, write down the events you are worrying about, what you are thinking about, and how you are feeling, so that you may become more aware of your anxiety feelings.

MY ANXIETY- PRODUCING SITUATION	THE THOUGHTS THAT GO THROUGH MY HEAD	HOW I FEEL WHEN THIS SITUATION HAPPENS

What trends do you see?

____

____

What steps can you take to reduce the thoughts that trigger your anxious feelings?

____

____

Nutrition and Anxiety

The relationship between nutrition and mood has been well documented. Certain foods and substances will create additional stress and anxiety. Substances that stress the body and enhance feelings of anxiety:

Caffeine	Alcohol	Salt	Red Meat
Nicotine	Candy	Sugar	Soda

Which of the above substances do you overdo?

____

____

____

How can you begin to consume less of these substances?

____

____

____

Foods that tend to reduce the symptoms of anxiety:

Fruits	Whole grain breads	Whole grain cereals
Vegetables	Brown rice	Nuts
Water	Fiber	Fish/Seafood

Which of the above foods would you consider adding to your regular diet?

____

____

____

How does anxiety affect your eating and drinking patterns?

____

____

____

Nutrition Log

In the log below, evaluate the amount of the substances listed you eat during a typical day.

Type of Food	Examples of the type of food	How Often?
Caffeine		
Nicotine		
Salt		
Red Meat		
Soda		
Sugar		
Candy		
Alcohol		

What did you realize by participating in this exercise?

____

____

____

____

Suppressed Feelings

People with anxiety issues tend to deliberately and consciously hold in their feelings.

This suppression can affect you in several ways:

- Cause you to have increased difficulty when you need to express your feelings
- Cause you to have difficulty in identifying your feelings
- Cause you to panic instead of dealing with your feelings

Verbalizing your emotions is part of understanding and regulating them. However, you may have been suppressing your emotions for so long that you aren't aware of what you are feeling. To be more mindful about your feelings, learning a method to describe your emotions will help to reduce their negativity.

For example:

When I feel scared, my stomach feels tied up in knots.

When I am happy, I feel energized and spiritual.

When I am worried, my muscles feel tense.

Emotions from a variety of sources can bring on feelings of anxiety:

1) **Intense feelings from the past**
Ex. (frustration) I am always the one who has to apologize in relationships.

2) **Feelings based on assumptions**
Ex. (lonely) I should not always, but I do, have to make the first move in my relationships.

3) **Feelings of anticipation about the future**
Ex. (fear I will look inadequate) I don't want to meet her friends next week because I know they won't accept me.

Which of these three sources affect you most? Why? How?

____

____

____

____

____

____

____

Feeling Observations and Descriptions

Think about the last week and record a stressful, anxiety producing event and how you felt, both positive and negative. Below, write about those feelings and the physical symptoms that accompanied those feelings.

WHAT HAPPENED?	DESCRIBE THOSE FEELINGS	HOW LONG DID THEY LAST?

What trends do you see?

____

____

____

Let Go of Your Feelings in a Healthy Way

It is important for you to learn ways to discharge your feelings physically and in a healthy way when you are feeling anxious. Some of these healthy ways are listed below. Place a check by those you already use.

- ❑ Physical workout
- ❑ House project
- ❑ Meditate
- ❑ Martial arts
- ❑ Yoga
- ❑ Garden
- ❑ Write
- ❑ Weight lift
- ❑ House clean
- ❑ Cook or bake
- ❑ Organize
- ❑ Walk or hike
- ❑ Other__________
- ❑ Other__________
- ❑ Other__________

Which of the methods you checked are the most and least effective for you?

Most effective: ____

____

Least effective: ____

____

Which of the other methods will you try? ______________________________

____

____

____

Express Your Feelings

People with anxiety problems tend to hold in their feelings and do not express them. Expressing your feelings is important in reducing the physical symptoms of anxiety. People who express their feelings assertively are able to let them go without hurting other people.

Ways you can express your feelings:

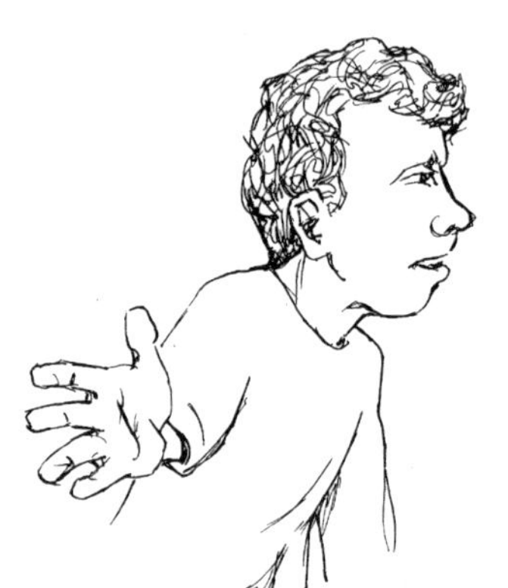

1) Share your feeling with someone you care about, one who must be . . .

- willing to listen actively to you
- trustworthy
- available when you need to express your feelings

2) Write your feelings in a journal if nobody is available to talk to:

- Keep a "feelings" journal of how you feel and what is underneath the feelings.
- Enter all of your feelings, making note of your strong feelings

- At the end of each week go back and review the feelings you wrote
- Identify broad patterns and themes in your strongest emotions.
- What seems to be triggering these intense emotions?
- Continue journaling

3) Have a good cry if needed!

Communicate Your Feelings

When you are having symptoms of anxiety, let other people know. When you are communicating your feelings, there are several rules to keep in mind:

- Use **I-Statements** such as "I feel…" or "I am feeling…" By using I-Statements, you take responsibility for your feelings. When you say "You make me feel…." you put your feelings off onto the other person and immediately put the other person on the defensive. No one makes us feel anything. We allow our feelings to happen.

  Now, try making I-Statements. Identify one or several people to whom you might like to relate your feelings. Practice below.

"I feel ____

when ____

____

____."

"I feel ____

when ____

____

____."

- Be certain the other person with whom you are communicating is able to **listen attentively**.
- Always take a **nonjudgmental** stance.
- Do not **blame** the other person.
- Check that the other person is **understanding** what you have said by asking simple questions like "Am I making sense to you?" or "Am I explaining it clearly?"
- Be **assertive** by being open, honest and direct.

ABCD's of Thinking Straight

Human beings are thinking, feeling and behaving beings. These four aspects interact when you are experiencing anxiety. To better understand the symptoms you are experiencing, it is important to explore how they develop.

Look at the following series of events that precede your anxiety symptoms:

A = An activating event

(I am doing a presentation at work next week)

LEADS TO

B = Your Thinking

(I will appear inadequate)

LEADS TO

C = Your Feelings

(I am afraid and anxious)

LEADS TO

D = Your physical symptoms

(I am having trouble breathing and I am tense)

How can you use this information next time to reduce your symptoms of anxiety?

____

____

____

____

____

____

____

____

Total-Body Relaxation

Anxiety manifests itself through physical symptoms in your body. These physical symptoms often reinforce your anxiety-producing thoughts and feelings. Total-Body Relaxation (often called Progressive Muscle Relaxation) is a simple technique used to stop anxiety by relaxing all of the muscles throughout your body, one group at a time.

Read through the following script several times before you attempt to do Total-Body Relaxation.

Take a few deep breaths, and begin to relax.

Get comfortable and put aside all of your worries.

Let each part of your body begin to relax…starting with your feet.

Imagine your feet relaxing as all of your tension begins to fade away.

Imagine the relaxation moving up into your calves and thighs . . . feel them beginning to relax.

Allow the relaxation to move into your lower back and stomach.

Your entire body from the waist down is now completely relaxed.

Continue now to let the relaxation move into your upper body.

Let go of any strain and discomfort you might feel.

Allow the relaxation to move into your chest until your chest feels completely relaxed.

Just enjoy the feeling of complete relaxation.

Continue to let the relaxation move through the muscles of your shoulders, then spread down into your upper arms, into your elbows, and finally all the way down to your wrists and hands.

Put aside all of your worries.

Let yourself be totally present in the moment and let yourself relax more and more. Let all the muscles in your neck unwind and let the relaxation move into your chin and jaws.

Feel the tension around your eyes flow away as the relaxation moves throughout your face and head.

Feel your forehead relax and your entire head beginning to feel lighter.

Let yourself drift deeper and deeper into relaxation and peace.

After you have read the above script several times, find a quiet location where you can practice Total-Body Relaxation. Assume a comfortable position in a chair. Take off your jewelry and glasses so that you are totally free. Try to let the relaxation happen without having to force it. If during the relaxation you lose concentration, don't be concerned, just begin again.

The Breath of Life

Your breathing generally illustrates the level of tension you are experiencing in your body.

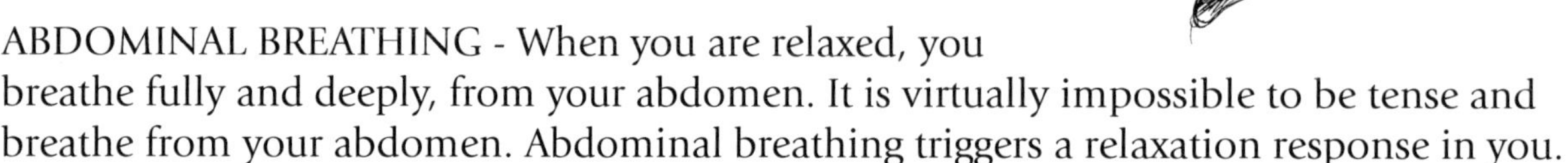

ABDOMINAL BREATHING - When you are relaxed, you breathe fully and deeply, from your abdomen. It is virtually impossible to be tense and breathe from your abdomen. Abdominal breathing triggers a relaxation response in you.

SHALLOW, CHEST-LEVEL BREATHING – When you are tense, your breathing usually becomes shallow and rapid, occurring high in your chest. With this type of breathing you tend to overbreathe and hyperventilate. If you breathe like this in certain situations, it's okay. You can retrain yourself to breathe deeply from your abdomen. Try this now:

ABDOMINAL BREATHING EXERCISE

Inhale slowly through your nose, down as deep as possible into your lungs. You should see your abdomen rise. When you have taken a full breath, pause for a moment and then exhale slowly through your nose or mouth. Be sure to exhale thoroughly.

Take ten of these full abdominal breaths. Keep your breaths as smooth and regular as possible. As you continue this process, you can try slowing your breathing rate. Pause for a second after each breath you take.

CALMING BREATH EXERCISE

If you feel a panic reaction coming on, try the Calming Breath exercise. Practice this so that you can use it if you need it.

Breathe from your abdomen, inhaling through your nose slowly to a count of five (count "one...two...three...four...five" as you inhale).

Pause and hold this breath for another count of five.

Slowly exhale through your nose or mouth to a count of five. Be sure that you exhale completely.

Wait for a few seconds, then repeat this process several more times.

Coping with My Anxiety

Table of Contents and Facilitator Notes

Ask for five participants. Ask each to read one of the steps, beginning at the bottom with number 1.

*Ex: **What situation makes you nervous?** (going to parties)*
What negative thoughts go through your mind about the situation?
(people will not like me, I will not have anyone to talk with, etc.)
What positive thoughts could you use to replace those negative thoughts?
(I am likeable, I am an interesting person to talk with, etc.)

Ask if any of the participants are willing to share a personal example of negative self-talk?

Ask if any of the participants are willing to share a personal example of positive self-talk?

Ask for participants who may like to read their Mental Imagery to the others. Initiate applause when each person finishes.

After handout is completed, ask participants to call out their favorite physical exercise and write these on a board. Suggest that they write good ideas that they are willing to consider on the back of their handout.

After handout is completed, ask participants to call out their best supports and write these on a board. Suggest that they write good ideas that they are willing to consider on the back of their handout.

After handout is completed, ask participants to call out their most enjoyable activities and write on a board. Suggest that they write good ideas that they are willing to consider on the back of their handout.

Table of Contents and Facilitator Notes

Reducing Anxiety – Creative Expression 88

After handout is completed, ask participants to call out their creative expressions and write on a board. Suggest that they write good ideas that they are willing to consider on the back of the back of their handout.

Assertive Styles 89

Ask participants to pair up after completing the worksheet. Choose an item from any one of the three styles, and then role-play. The other participants can guess which style they are portraying: passive, assertive or aggressive.

Nurture Yourself 90

After completing the handout, ask the participants to name the nurturing activities they wrote on the blank lines. Ask for a show of hands if other participants would be interested in named activities.

Exercising 91

Before using this handout, ask the participants the reasons they don't exercise. Excuses used most often:

"I don't have time."
"I'm too old"
"Exercise is boring"
"It is inconvenient"
"It hurts"
"I'm too tired"
"It won't help"

After using the handout, process ways to combat these excuses.

Time Management 92

After discussing the handout, and the participants have completed the questions at the bottom of the page, ask if they would like to share some of the items they do well at home or work.

My Success Story 93

Example: Tell a story about a time when you usually would be anxious about an event or a situation, but this time you were not.

I needed to speak at a meeting and ordinarily I get very anxious.

What changed? Why was it different?

I knew the subject matter well.

What did you do differently to feel less anxious.

I told myself that I could answer questions easily and if I didn't know, I would say so.

Three Wishes 94

Participants may be willing to share some of their wishes.

Coping with My Anxiety Scale Introduction

To live to your full potential you need to learn to cope with your anxiety. Coping has been described as the efforts you use to manage specific internal and external stressors in an effort to solve personal and interpersonal problems and to master and reduce anxiety.

People use many different strategies to cope with anxiety. All of the strategies have advantages and disadvantages. This assessment is designed to help you understand how effective you are in preventing and coping with anxiety.

Read each statement carefully. Circle the number of the response that shows how descriptive each statement is of you. Please answer all the questions honestly, using the following scale:

3 = True **2 = Somewhat True** **1 = Not True**

In the following example, the circled 2 indicates that the statement is **Somewhat True** of the person completing the scale.

In handling my anxiety . . .

I do a reasonable job of coping 3 (2) 1

This is not a test and there are no right or wrong answers. Do not spend too much time thinking about your answers. Your initial response will be the most true for you.
Be sure to respond to every statement.

Name ____ **Date** ______________

Turn to the next page and begin.

Scale: Coping with My Anxiety

3 = True 2 = Somewhat True 1 = Not True

In handling my anxiety . . .

I do a reasonable job of coping	3	2	1
I know how to reduce my anxiety	3	2	1
I know how to react if I begin to panic	3	2	1
I am able to confront my mistaken beliefs	3	2	1
I know the nutritious foods to eat to reduce effects of my anxiety	3	2	1
I have a support system to help manage my anxiety	3	2	1
I am assertive when I need to be	3	2	1
I can easily monitor and correct my self-talk	3	2	1
I use visualizations to help reduce stress and anxiety	3	2	1
I use relaxation techniques to relax my body	3	2	1
I take care of myself and my personal needs	3	2	1
I am comfortable saying "no" when I need to	3	2	1
I do not need approval from others	3	2	1
I do not try to live up to the expectations of others	3	2	1
I do not back down when others are overpowering or stubborn	3	2	1
I manage my stress well	3	2	1
I do not question my worth as a human being	3	2	1
I do not worry about being rejected by others	3	2	1
I am not overly sensitive of critical statements from others	3	2	1
I rarely try to control things I cannot control	3	2	1
I try to nurture myself when I feel anxious	3	2	1
I work on maintaining my self-esteem	3	2	1
I drink only the liquids that do not add to my anxiety	3	2	1
I have meaning and purpose in my life	3	2	1
I look to my religious and spiritual beliefs which helps me	3	2	1

TOTAL = __________

GO TO THE SCORING DIRECTIONS

Scale: Coping with My Anxiety Scoring Directions

This scale is designed to help you understand how effective you are in coping with your anxiety.

Scoring the Coping with My Anxiety Scale:

Add the numbers you circled on the scale and write that score on the line marked TOTAL. Then transfer that total to the space below:

Coping With My Anxiety Total = __________

Profile Interpretation

Individual Scales Score	Result	Indications
59 to 75	high	If you score in the high range, you tend to be effective in coping with your anxiety.
42 to 58	moderate	If you score in the moderate range, you have some skills in coping with your anxiety.
25 to 41	low	If you score in the low range, you tend to have difficulty in coping with your anxiety.

No matter how you scored, low, moderate or high, you will benefit from these exercises.

Steps to Conquer Anxiety

Below is a set of steps that you can use to reduce your feelings of anxiety and begin to effectively cope with those feelings.

These steps are designed to help you cope with anxiety from its onset. Begin at the bottom step, number 1, and proceed up the steps.

5. **Readjust Emotions** – Lastly, you need to identify, express, and regulate your emotions. Practice positive thinking and self-talk, and notice how your emotions change.

4. **Think Realistically** – Next you need to realistically assess the accuracy and rationality of your thoughts. Identify which type of negative self-talk you are using.

3. **Redefine Physical Panic Symptoms** – Now, begin calming your body and achieve a sense of deep relaxation. Tell yourself, *"I must unclench my fists, take deep, slow breaths, progressively tighten, then relax my muscles."*

2. **Rationally Interpret Bodily Symptoms** – Next, you need to interpret the physical symptoms you are experiencing. Tell yourself, *"My sweating, dizziness, nausea or other symptoms are just my body's over-reaction to a perceived threat."*

1. **Reduce Physical Tension** – Begin to cope with anxiety by first recognizing and understanding the physical symptoms that warn of anxiety. Tell yourself, *"I realize I have clenched teeth, tight muscles, quick shallow breaths, rapid heartbeat, etc.*

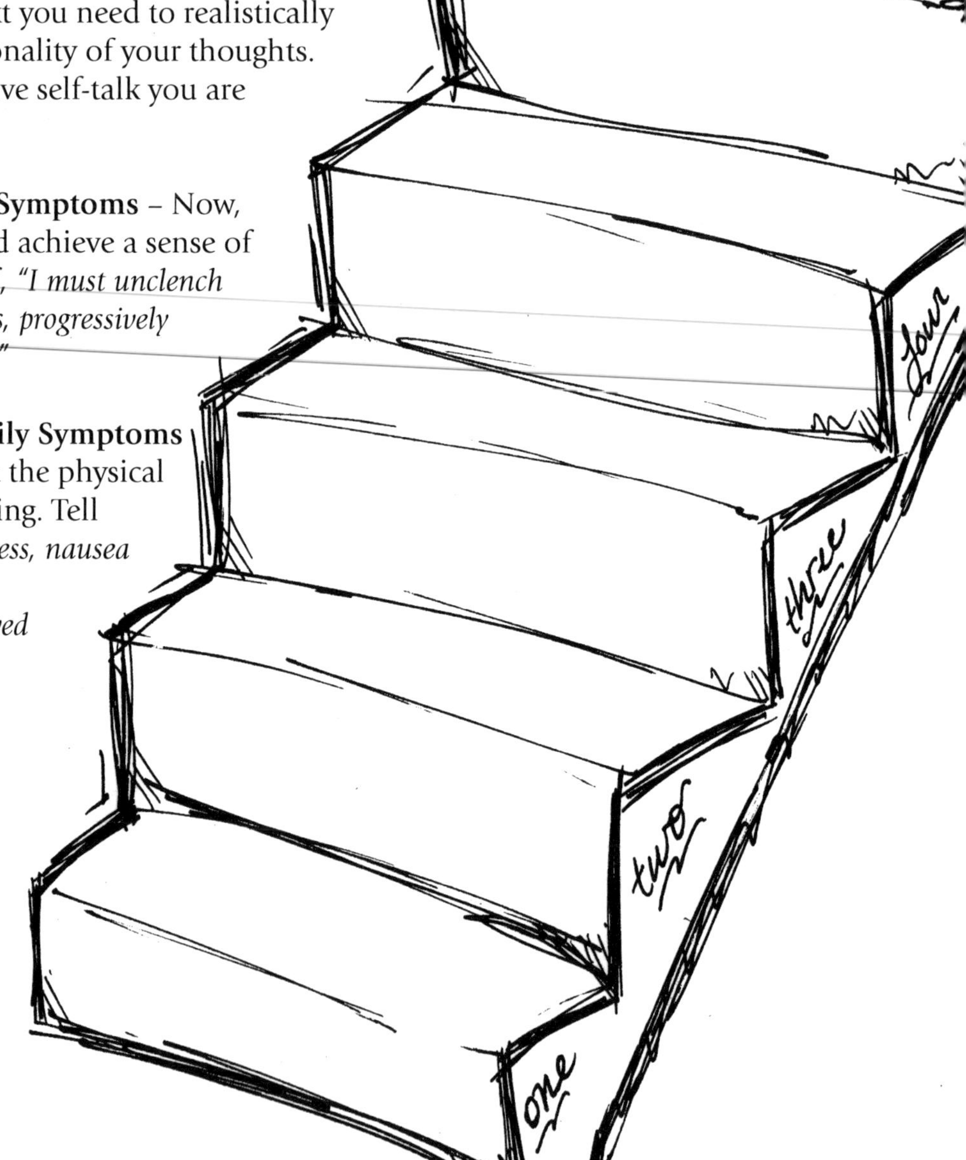

Your Thoughts

Your thoughts greatly influence the amount of anxiety you feel. Think about a situation in which you feel anxious. Then identify the thoughts and images that keep running through your head related to this situation.

In what situation do you feel very anxious?

What negative thoughts and images go through your mind about this situation?

What positive thoughts and images could you use to replace those negative thoughts?

Types of Negative Self-Talk

**Negative self-talk usually takes one of three forms.
Think about the type of self-talk that tends to be present in your life.
Then list some of the negative things you say to yourself.**

Worriers ***say, "What if..."***

"What if I don't do well at the game..."

"What if I say something stupid..."

Now you try it. List some things you say to yourself when you are worrying:

____

____

____

Perfectionists ***say, "I should..." and "I must..."***

"I must get the job..."

"I should be loved by everyone..."

Now you try it. List some perfectionistic things you say to yourself:

____

____

____

Critics ***say, "I can't do this..."***

"I can't go back to school at my age..."

"I can't start my own business..."

Now you try it. List some critical things you say to yourself:

____

____

____

Types of Positive Self-Talk

Negative self-talk can be turned into positive self-talk.
Think about the type of negative self-talk that tends to be present in your life.
Then list some of the positive statements you can change it to.

Worriers ***say, "What if..."***

"What if I don't do well at the game..." can be changed to "All I can do is the best I am capable of."

"What if I say something stupid..." can be changed to *"I can't control what others think or say."*

Now you try it. List some things you say to yourself when you are worrying and turn them into positives:

____

____

____

Perfectionists ***say, "I should..." and "I must..."***

"I must get the job..." can be changed to *"If I don't get the job, I'll look for another one."*

"I should be loved by everyone..." can be changed to *"I'm lovable, but not everyone loves everyone!."*

Now you try it. List some perfectionistic things you say to yourself and turn them into positives:

____

____

____

Critics ***say, "I can't do this..."***

"I can't go back to school at my age..." can be changed to *"I can still concentrate and learn!"*

"I can't start my own business..." can be changed to *"I am as smart and persistent as others who have started their own businesses."*

Now you try it. List some critical things you say to yourself and turn them into positives:

____

____

____

Using Mental Imagery

Working with images can be a useful way to reduce anxiety. Mental Imagery is the use of memories of visual events to project a mental picture in your mind.

Here is an example:

I picture myself in the forest that backed up to my childhood home. When I begin to feel anxious I can project myself back to those woods and begin to feel relaxed. I just close my eyes and picture myself walking into those woods. I notice how beautiful the trees appear and the sounds of the birds singing. I imagine walking through the tall trees with their various shades of leaves. I smell the fresh air and the scent of evergreen. With each breath I take I imagine breathing in the beautiful, vivid colors that are present. This is my personal paradise."

Now, write out a pleasant imagery scene, one that you will like picturing and remembering. When you find yourself in an anxiety-producing situation, you can focus on this scene.

____

____

____

____

____

____

____

____

____

____

____

____

____

Reducing Anxiety with Physical Exercise

You can use many distractions to reduce anxiety before it spirals into a heightened, debilitating state. These distractions allow you to focus on things outside of yourself. Physical exercise is one of the most powerful tools for reducing anxiety because it directly impacts the physiological and psychological factors that underlie anxiety.

What are your favorite exercises and how often do you participate in them?

____

____

____

____

What sports do you like to play and how often do you participate in them?

____

____

____

____

What are some chores around the house that provide good exercise and how often do you participate in them?

____

____

____

____

What are some things you do, or could do in your community to get exercise?

____

____

____

____

Reducing Anxiety with a Support System

Conversation is an excellent way to shift your focus away from your worries or to talk about those worries with trusted people. By developing a support system of those to whom you can talk when you feel anxious, you are developing one of the most powerful tools for reducing anxiety.

With whom can you talk or be with, that distracts you from your anxieties?

____

____

____

____

With whom do you like to discuss your concerns?

____

____

____

____

What qualities do those people have that allows you to confide in them?

____

____

____

____

Who else might you add to your support system list, people who have some of the same qualities you described above?

____

____

____

____

Reducing Anxiety with Enjoyable Activities

Enjoyable activities help to replenish your energy when it is waning. They lift up your spirit. They are those recreation-time experiences in which you have fun and engage in play. These activities can be done alone or with other people.

What activities do you like to do that bring you a sense of relaxation?

____

____

____

What activities do you enjoy so much that you lose your sense of time?

____

____

____

What are your favorite hobbies and leisure activities?

____

____

____

What activities do you feel passionate about?

____

____

____

Which ones bring you meaning and a sense of purpose?

____

____

____

Reducing Anxiety with Creative Expression

Creative expression can include a variety of activities including drawing, painting, writing, journaling, gardening, making jewelry, arts and crafts, music, singing and dancing, acting, wood-working, graphic arts. Express yourself creatively – the possibilities are endless – just use your imagination.

How do you express your creativity?

____

____

____

____

What was the last thing you did that was creative?

____

____

____

____

What creative activity would you like to do more often? Why don't you?

____

____

____

____

In what areas of your life do you feel you can be more creative?

____

____

____

____

Assertive Styles

Being assertive by asking for what you want in an honest, open and direct communication style. Refusing to do things just to please people, is important in reducing your anxiety.

Check the communications styles below that best describes you.

The Passive Style

- ❑ I let other people always get their way
- ❑ I don't express my feelings
- ❑ I feel guilty when I ask for what I want
- ❑ I want to please other people
- ❑ I don't tell others what I need

The Aggressive Style

- ❑ I am demanding about what I want
- ❑ I am insensitive to what others want
- ❑ I attempt to get what I want at all costs
- ❑ I act in a hostile way toward others
- ❑ I am intimidating at times

The Assertive Style

- ❑ I ask for what I want in a simple, open and direct manner
- ❑ I communicate my needs honestly
- ❑ I stand up for myself
- ❑ I say "no" when I don't want to do something
- ❑ Other people know where I stand

In what situations can you begin to act more assertively?

____

____

____

____

____

Nurture Yourself

By taking a time-out, you can reduce anxiety through small acts of kindness toward yourself on a daily basis. Allow yourself to make time each day to nurture yourself, away from your duties at work and home. When you nurture yourself you begin to develop a loving relationship with you!

Some of the nurturing activities you can engage in for yourself are listed below. Place a check mark in the box by those you already do, or plan to do, and then list others in the blank lines.

- ❑ Take a walk
- ❑ Take a long bubble bath
- ❑ Go to a matinee movie
- ❑ Meditate
- ❑ Watch a sunset
- ❑ Watch children play
- ❑ Plant a garden
- ❑ Listen to favorite music
- ❑ Play with a pet
- ❑ Do yoga
- ❑ Read a mystery novel
- ❑ Drink a cup of tea
- ❑ Take a class
- ❑ ____________________
- ❑ ____________________
- ❑ ____________________
- ❑ ____________________
- ❑ ____________________
- ❑ ____________________
- ❑ ____________________
- ❑ Get a massage
- ❑ Read an inspirational book
- ❑ Work on a crossword puzzle
- ❑ Write in a journal
- ❑ Go to a local park
- ❑ Visit friends
- ❑ Rent and watch videos
- ❑ Browse in a bookstore
- ❑ Ride a horse
- ❑ Visit a museum
- ❑ Learn a foreign language
- ❑ Play computer games
- ❑ Play chess
- ❑ ____________________
- ❑ ____________________
- ❑ ____________________
- ❑ ____________________
- ❑ ____________________
- ❑ ____________________
- ❑ ____________________

Exercising

Regular exercise is one of the most effective ways to reduce anxiety. Exercise has been shown to reduce anxiety and phobic experiences, insomnia and depression, and to enhance feelings of well-being and self-esteem.

Several ways you can exercise are listed below. Put a check mark next to those you already do. Draw a stick figure of yourself in the box next to any that you will try soon.

Lifting Weights or Aerobic Exercises		**Martial Arts or Yoga**	
Hiking or Walking		**Yard Work or Gardening**	
Cycling or Swimming		**Running or Jogging**	
Other ____________		**Other** ____________	

Before you begin to exercise, remember to check with your medical doctor to make sure you are physically able.

Time Management

How you manage your time, and then find more time for fun and relaxation can play a huge part in how you manage anxiety. To assist you in being certain that you are doing enough to maintain a healthy and relaxed lifestyle, here are some suggestions:

AT HOME

- Give yourself time each day to rejuvenate and replenish your energy.
- Get enough sleep each night.
- How many hours do you normally sleep each night? ______________________
- Take time each day to stop doing things and simply rest.
- When and how can you relax during the day? ______________________
- Devote time each day to your relationships.
- Take a daytime nap if possible.
- Be sure to "be" each day, rather than "do." (We are human 'beings, not human doings'!)
- Take time to lie on the couch and do nothing.
- Allow yourself to be non-productive a little while of each day.
- Spend time having fun.
- What do you like to do for recreation and fun? ______________________
- Spend time alone each day. Reflect, read, meditate, etc.
- If you are a workaholic, take time to enjoy non-work aspects of your life.
- How can you stream-line your life. What unnecessary activities can you delegate or eliminate? ______________________

AT WORK

- Prioritize work by differentiating between essential and non-essential tasks.
- Delegate work to others when appropriate.
- Allow extra time to complete tasks if possible.
- Know that it's okay if your work is not perfect at times.
- Don't feel like your work has to be perfect at all times.
- Plan work tasks so that you can eliminate the "deadline crunch."
- Be assertive and say "no" if you think it's the right thing to do.
- Manage your time as well as possible during the work day to avoid bringing work home or working overtime.

Which of these do you do well? ______________________

____

Which of these do you not do so well?______________________

____

My Success Story

Tell a story about a time when you usually would be anxious about an event or a situation, but this time you were not.

What changed? Why was it different?

What did you do differently to be less anxious?

Three Wishes

A genie has just given you a magic lamp, and told you that you can wish for anything you like related to your fears or anxieties.

If you had three wishes that would be granted to you to help you deal with your fears and anxieties, what would these wishes be?

Wish #1 ______________________________

____

____

Wish #2 ______________________________

____

____

Wish #3 ______________________________

____

____

What can you now do to begin to make these wishes come true?

Wish #1 ______________________________

____

____

Wish #2 ______________________________

____

____

Wish #3 ______________________________

____

____

Whole Person Associates is the leading publisher of training resources for professionals who empower people to create and maintain healthy lifestyles. Our creative resources will help you work effectively with your clients in the areas of stress management, wellness promotion, mental health and life skills.

Please visit us at our web site: **www.wholeperson.com**. You can check out our entire line of products, place an order, request our print catalog, and sign up for our monthly special notifications.

Whole Person Associates

800-247-6789